Ancient Mysteries

by David Orme

Trailblazers

Ancient Mysteries
by David Orme
Educational consultant: Helen Bird

Illustrated by Ulises Roman

Published by Ransom Publishing Ltd.
51 Southgate Street, Winchester, Hants. SO23 9EH
www.ransom.co.uk

ISBN   978 184167 801 6

First published in 2009

Copyright © 2009 Ransom Publishing Ltd.

Illustrations copyright © 2009 Ulises Roman
'Get the Facts' section - images copyright: volcano - Jesús Javier del Valle Melendo; big wave - Paul Topp; Nazca lines - Jarno Gonzalez Zarraonandia; Great Pyramid of Khufu - Luke Daniek; Great Pyramid diagram - Jeff Dahl; Easter Island - Andrzej Gibasiewicz, John Snelgrove, Marcelo Kohn; skull - Ian Knox; Yeti scalp - Nuno Nogueira; big foot - Ronnie Sampson, Chris Brock; demon - Anthony Taylor; terracotta warriors - Christine Gonsalves, Boris Shapiro; cave couple - Dennis Cox; aeroplane with banner - Russell Tate; Pharaoh - Cruz Puga.

Ancient Mysteries

Contents

Get the facts   **5**

Atlantis   6
The Nazca lines   7
The Great Pyramid of Khufu   8
Bog men   10
Easter Island   11
Yeti and Big Foot   12
Ancient maps and aeroplanes   14
Shi Huangdi's tomb   16

Fiction

Doorway to Demons   19

Ancient Mysteries word check   **36**

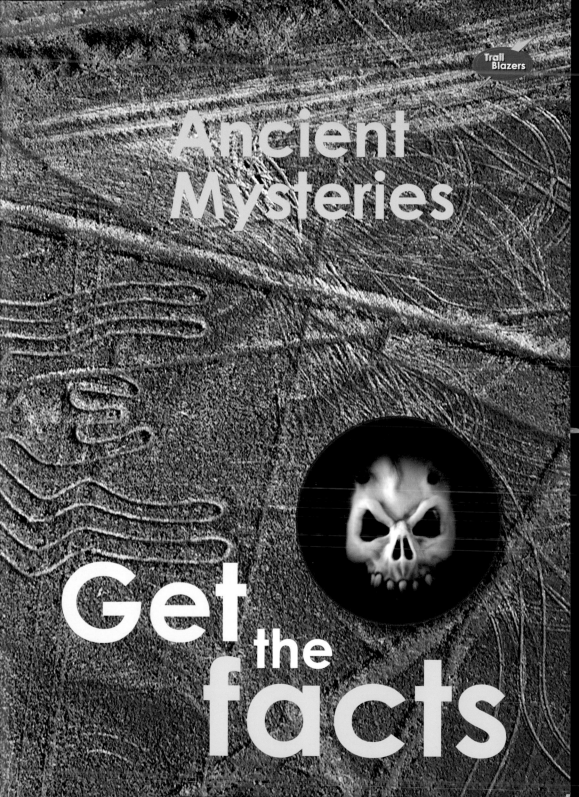

Ancient Mysteries

Trail Blazers

Get the facts

Atlantis

An ancient story says there was an island called **Atlantis**. It was in the middle of the Atlantic Ocean. Life was perfect for everyone on the island.

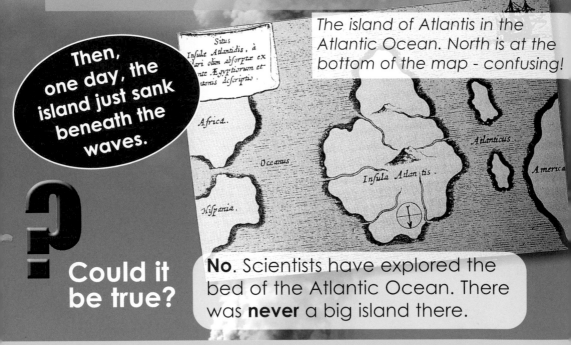

The island of Atlantis in the Atlantic Ocean. North is at the bottom of the map - confusing!

Then, one day, the island just sank beneath the waves.

Could it be true?

No. Scientists have explored the bed of the Atlantic Ocean. There was **never** a big island there.

So that's that, then?

Well, maybe not. Over 2,500 years ago, a volcano erupted in the Mediterranean Sea. This caused a great wave called a **tsunami**.

Many thousands of people would have been killed. This could have been how the legend started.

The Nazca lines

The Nazca lines are not a legend – they are real, and amazing!

Where are they?

In a desert in **Peru**, **South America**. There are hundreds of figures showing animals such as monkeys, llamas and spiders. Some of the figures are over 250 metres long!

How were they made?

The desert is covered with dark stones. Around 2,000 years ago, people starting moving them so the light soil underneath would show up.

So what's the mystery?

1. Why did they do it?
2. You can't really see the figures from the ground. But of course the people who made them didn't have aeroplanes! Er ...

A theory

Some people think it is an alien space port. *But how would pictures of animals help you land a flying saucer?*

The Great Pyramid of Khufu

This great pyramid was built over **four and a half thousand years ago**. It is made of around two and a half million heavy blocks of stone.

Somebody worked out that if you tried to build it today, using modern cranes, it would take at least **twenty-five years** to finish it.

Somehow, the Egyptians managed it in about 23 years!

Are there any more mysteries about the great pyramid?

There is one big mystery left.

There are two rooms in the pyramid, called the **King's Chamber** and the **Queen's Chamber**.

They both have **tiny tunnels** leading upwards from them. They are too small for a person to get through.

King's Chamber

Queen's Chamber

A **robot** was sent up the tunnel from the Queen's Chamber.

It found – a tiny door!

So what's on the other side of the door?

That's the mystery!

?

Bog men

This guy might look peaceful, but he came to a nasty end – around 2,000 years ago!

He is known as Tollund Man and he was found in a bog in Denmark.

Because bogs are very acid, bodies don't rot. The skin is turned into a sort of leather.

Over 1,000 bog bodies have been found. Many of them were murdered before they were thrown into the bog. Tollund Man has a rope around his neck.

Why did they do that?

It's another mystery. Maybe he was a criminal – or maybe he was a **human sacrifice!**

Easter Island

Easter Island is a very lonely place in the **Pacific Ocean**.

It was a tough place to live.

Yet around 600 years ago, the islanders found time to carve and set up nearly 900 huge stone statues around the island.

Some of them weigh over 75 tons!

How did they move them?

Probably with ropes and wooden sledges. When the trees on the island disappeared, they stopped building statues.

Why did the trees die out?

Maybe because of climate change, or because the islanders cut down too many of them.

Yeti and Big Foot

Yeti

The Yeti is supposed to be a huge, hairy creature with red fur that lives in the Himalayan mountains of Nepal and Tibet.

> **Does it really exist?**

Well, in 1970 a strange, ape-like creature was seen hanging around a climbers' camp.

And here's a picture of a Yeti scalp.

Is it a fake?

PROBABLY

Big Foot

Big Foot is another big, hairy apeman. It is supposed to live in the forests of North America.

> **Well, does it?**

Well, this time, there's a photograph, and even a movie!

Hang on!

That looks just like someone wearing a monkey suit!

Well, yes, and here's a funny coincidence. The photo was taken just after they made a movie called

What do scientists say about the Yeti and Big Foot?

They don't believe in them.
(Well, most of them don't.)

The Shug Monkey

Another mysterious creature is the

The Shug Monkey runs along roads at night in , England.

What does shug mean? It means demon. Where's the evidence that it exists? There isn't any.

So it doesn't really exist then?

NO.

Ancient maps and aeroplanes

This map was drawn in **1513** by a map maker from Turkey called **Piri Reis**. It was lost for years, then found again in **1929**.

People who studied the map were amazed to see **Antarctica** on it. Antarctica wasn't discovered until **1820**!

Piri said he had made his map partly from copying other very old maps.

Some people think this shows that ancient people explored the world thousands of years ago. They may even have had aeroplanes!

REALLY?

Probably not. Other people say Piri put a continent on the south of his map because people guessed there was one there – to balance the big continents of the north.

They even had a name for it – '**unknown southern land**'.

Er ... good name!

But the mystery isn't quite solved. The **coastline** he drew looks very much like – the coast of **Antarctica**!

Talking of aircraft ...

This object was found in an ancient tomb in Egypt.

Some **archaeologists** say it is a model of a bird.

Others say it is a toy model of an **aircraft** that is missing a tail fin.

Fly Pharaoh airlines!

WHAT DO YOU THINK?

15

Shi Huangdi's tomb

In 1974 a farmer digging a well in China found a strange statue, made of **terracotta** (baked clay). Archaeologists started to dig, and found over 8,000 more of them!

The Emperor Qin Shi Huangdi wanted to carry on capturing other countries after he was dead! He thought that the figures would become an army in the afterlife. They even had weapons and horses.

Was Shi Huangdi a good emperor?

In many ways he was, but if he didn't like you, he buried you alive!

Shi Huangdi – not friendly.

So what's the mystery?

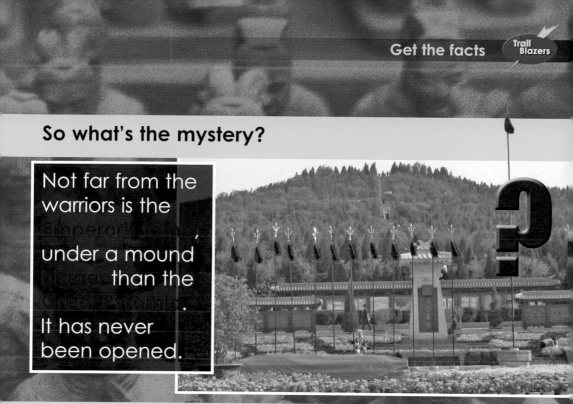

Not far from the warriors is the Emperor's tomb, under a mound bigger than the Great Pyramid. It has never been opened.

So why don't they dig it up?

The tomb is said to be a complete city, full of precious jewels. There is even a complete map of China, with rivers of flowing mercury, a liquid metal.

The tomb is said to be **booby trapped**. Anyone who goes in will be shot by **crossbows**!

No one knows if it is true, but there is one clue. When they checked the soil of the mound, they found – **mercury**.

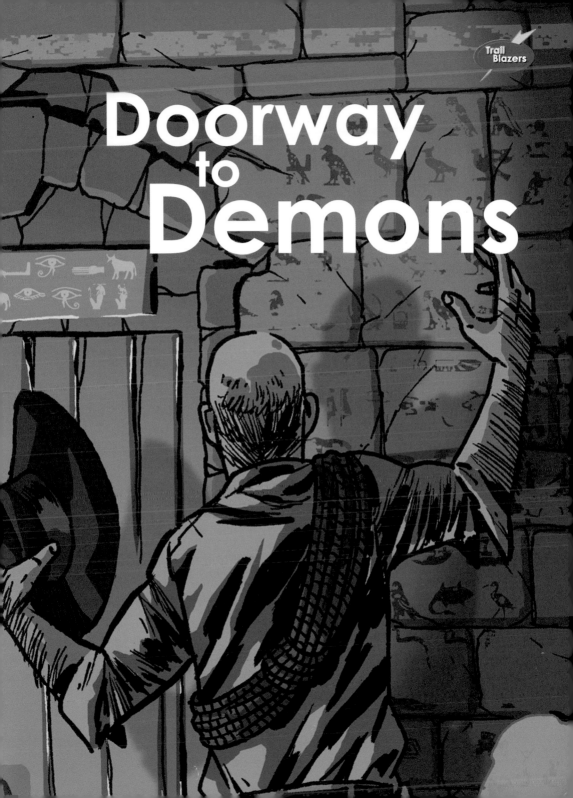

Chapter 1:
The wall

'I'm sure there is something behind this!'

Sir Giles Topping, the archaeologist, stared at the wall.

'Why do you say that?'

'These stones aren't part of the wall of this tomb. They've been piled up against the wall. There must be something hidden there!'

At first, the new tomb had been a disappointment for Sir Giles and his assistant Peter. It was empty. It didn't really seem like a tomb at all. But now there was a mystery to solve!

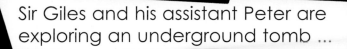

Sir Giles and his assistant Peter are exploring an underground tomb ...

I'm sure there is something hidden behind this!

The blocks of stone were huge. The archaeologists wondered how the builders had got them into place without machines to help them.

After a lot of hard work, they got some of the stones shifted.

'Sir Giles! You are right! Look, there is a doorway!' shouted Peter.

Sir Giles was thrilled. This could be the discovery that would make him famous!

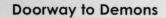

Chapter 2:
The warning

At last, all the blocks were moved.

But the door was solid stone, and there didn't seem to be any way to open it. How were they going to get through?

Peter was worried about something else. Above the door he found some ancient writing.

'Sir Giles! Look at this! It's a warning!'

Then Peter found something ...
Sir Giles! This says there is a world of demons on the other side of the door!

'What does it say?'

'Beware! This door must remain sealed! Beyond is another world – the world of demons!'

Sir Giles scratched the long, white scar on his right cheek.

'World of demons? What nonsense! That's just there to frighten people off – but it doesn't frighten me! There may be treasure behind that door – and I'm going to find it!'

But getting through the door wasn't going to be easy.

That doesn't frighten me. There may be treasure through that door!

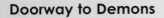

Chapter 3:
'I can hear something!'

Sir Giles was going to break through the door himself. Only *he* was going to have the glory of finding an amazing treasure.

He got a hammer and chisel and started work.

The stone was very hard, and at first he hardly made a mark on the door. But at last the stone began to fall away in large flakes. The sound of his hammering echoed all around the empty tomb.

'Sir Giles! Stop for a moment! I'm sure I can hear something!'

Sir Giles glared round. He didn't want to stop!

'I can't hear anything. You must be imagining it!'

He picked up his hammer and chisel again, ready to start work on the door. Then he heard the sound himself. A muffled hammering.

It was coming from the other side of the door.

Then Sir Giles heard it too. Hammering – from the other side of the door!

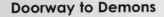

Chapter 4:
The world of the demons

Peter was really frightened now.

'Sir Giles! You must stop! It's the world of demons!'

'I told you, that's all nonsense!' roared Sir Giles, and he started hammering even harder.

A great chunk of stone fell away, leaving a hole big enough to climb through. Someone was standing there, looking through at him.

Sir Giles knew that face. It was his.

Both Sir Giles's fell back in amazement.

'You're ... me! From another world! Are you an archaeologist too?'

'That's right!'

'So ... I've found another world!'

The other Sir Giles climbed through the hole.

'No you haven't. *I* have.'

Peter gasped when he saw the new Sir Giles stab *his* Sir Giles in the chest.

'You **are** from the world of demons!' he said.

The new Sir Giles turned towards Peter with the knife.

Then Peter noticed something. This Sir Giles's scar was on his left cheek, not his right.

You're me! I've found another world!
No you haven't. *I* have.
You ***are*** from the world of demons!

Ancient Mysteries word check

afterlife	legend
alien	mercury
Antarctica	Nazca lines
archaeologist	pyramid
Atlantic	sacrifice
Big Foot	Shug Monkey
booby trap	statue
climate change	terracotta
Egyptain	tomb
emperor	tsunami
flying saucer	volcano
Himalayan	warrior
human sacrifice	Yeti
Khufu	